What The Silence Didn't Say

Yusha Rizvi

BookLeaf Publishing

India | USA | UK

Made with ❤ on the BookLeaf Publishing Platform
www.bookleafpub.in
www.bookleafpub.com

Dedication

This book is for those who have felt too deeply, loved too fiercely, and lost too painfully.

For the restless souls who find comfort in the silence of the night and the weight of their own thoughts.

For the ones who have searched for meaning in heartbreak and strength in solitude.

And most of all, for those who still dare to feel—this is for you.

Preface

I never set out to be a poet. I never sat down with the intention of writing about love, loss, or the restless thoughts that keep me awake at night. But somewhere along the way, words became my refuge. Every poem in this collection is a piece of me—born in quiet moments, shaped by emotions too heavy to carry, and set free on these pages.

This book is not just poetry; it is my journey. A journey through love that once felt eternal, the sting of heartbreak, the weight of loneliness, and the quiet hope that refuses to fade. It's about questioning everything—time, fate, even God—because sometimes, the only way to find answers is to ask the hardest questions.

You may find yourself in these words, or maybe you'll just hear the echoes of my voice. Either way, if this book makes you feel *something*, then I have done what I set out to do.

So, read these poems not as perfectly crafted verses, but as raw confessions. Read them as whispers from a soul that, just like yours, is still searching, still healing, still holding on.

Welcome to my world.

Acknowledgements

This book would not have been possible without the moments of solitude, the sleepless nights, and the unspoken emotions—without you, these poems would never have been born.

To every reader who chooses to step into these pages, thank you for allowing my emotions to become a part of your journey.

1. Where Love Resides

If I ever encountered beauty, it was in you.
If I was ever hypnotized, it was by your eyes.
If I ever felt healed, it was through your touch.
If I ever knew euphoria, it was in your vibe.
Have I ever felt the same? I couldn't decide-
Until I saw you and realized,
This is where I will finally reside.
Should I call it love, or let you decide?
Will you hold my hand for the rest of my life?

2. Chasing Time, Chasing Love

Has time stopped, or is it moving too fast?
Will love fade away, or will it last?
What are these doubts in my head, the pain in my heart?
Is it the hand of God or burden of the past?

Maybe I am close, maybe I am lost.
This *faith* I will keep—salvation or not.
And time will wait, the chase will end,
For I will find it—no matter the cost.

3. Hold My Hand

My insecurities whisper what isn't there,
I know my flaws, all I ask is care.
When I speak the truth my heart must share,
Don't turn away—just stay, just hear.
If you hold my hand instead of letting me go,
My fears will fade, and love will grow.

4. Testimony of Love

Close your eyes, and I'll be there beside you,
You're the one I cherish among the few.
I know I am old, but you make me feel new,
This is my testimony of love, not just a point of view.

5. A Night to Remember

I see myself walking this street, your hand in mine,
Smoking a cigarette, on our way to the bar then sipping
on the wine.
Tipsy but not tired, we'll reach the beach by nine,
Ending the night on the sand, beneath the moon's shine.

6. Never Let Go

I may let you leave, but I'll never let you go.
Love, why do you pull me in, then strike me with one
blow?
You lift me high, then cast me low,
Please don't leave this time—just end my woe.

7. Betrayed Devotion

I hate my heart—it keeps lying to me,
Swearing love is true, that they're trying for me.
I mended their wings, yet they won't fly for me,
They crushed my hope, then built a shrine for me.

8. Where I Do Not Belong

I am still where you left me, lost in the past,
But I guess you moved on, found peace at last.
I am no longer the first on your mind,
Yet I wonder—was I ever, or was I just blind?
I search for answers, but silence is strong,
What did I do? Where did I go wrong?
I crave the truth, yet fear its weight,
For I am not strong enough to carry fate.
Perhaps you've found a home so warm,
A place untouched by love's old storm.
And there you stand, steady and free,
While here I fade, where I no longer should be.

9. Lost in the Rain

I am leaving—you will never find me again.
You robbed me with love, left me with pain.
Where did I go wrong? Was my love in vain?
While I sheltered you, you left me crying in the rain.

10. River of Tears

I woke up with a dream—but it turned to despair,
Standing before her—yet she didn't care.
I called her name, but no one could hear,
Loneliness swallowed me—then came the tears.

From the bottom of my heart, to the end of my eyes,
They flowed like a river—a river of plight.
And I danced to its tune,
Like a song of silent cries.

11. Standstill

All of my life has come to a standstill,
Is this the end or just the end of my will?
The doctor says all I need are the meds,
If that's true, I'll pay the bills.
Why? Why is it like that?
That I hate my life as if it's bad.
They say I don't know how to live,
That my world is different—as if I'm mad.
Hear me out! I just want to live the way I dream,
Where I can hear myself, not my screams.
Sadness is fine, but I wouldn't mind joy in between,
I wish you could look in my eyes and know what I mean.
Till then, my life remains at a standstill,
With too much time left to fill.
Cigarettes will be my warmth and my hope,
That life is waiting—just beyond the hill.

12. 4 AM Solitude

I'm moving in circles—tears and sorrow,
Chasing the past, drowning in tomorrow.
It's 4 AM, a cigarette burns slow,
Alone in the dark, feeling hollow.
Sleepless nights, wet eyes, a bed like gallows,
Echoes of love lost, wrapped in shadows.
Wish I could see you just once again,
Till then, meet **Solitude**—my only friend, whispering
hello.

13. Regrets

Do I have any regrets,
As I sit here, smoking cigarettes?
No one can answer this for me,
Then when will I figure it?

As days repeats with endless nights.
My thoughts on loop, trying to fight.
"Burn the past"—I heard a cry.
"From ashes and smoke, you will rise".

14. Devoted to Sorrow

Oh, Sadness, why do you cling to me so tight?
It hurts—my tears fall endlessly each night.
The past haunts me, a ghost I cannot fight.
My world is burning; don't try to make it right.

Oh, Sadness, why don't you take a break,
So that I can talk with my pain without the ache.
Sinking in devotion to this endless lake.
Drowning in these thoughts, maybe I can wake.

15. The Cost of a Heart

Beaten to pulp and bleeding,
Alone, yet still standing.
It wasn't the fight, but life itself,
That tore a piece of me—yet I survived.
Neither I won, nor I lost,
For having a heart—that was the cost.
Asking for directions, but who do I trust?
What I seek doesn't exist—what exists is all dust.

16. Will You Remember Me?

If I'm gone one day, will you remember me?

Like you do now, or will I fade away?

Will I be forgotten, as if I never existed,

Or will you hold me in your heart, come what may?

If heaven is real, will I find you there?

Like I found you once before.

Will I ever see you again,

Or will I be left wandering, forever unsure?

Tell me now—before it's too late.

They say for souls like mine, there's a place.

Where I can close my eyes just once,

And become one with the fire and be done with the chase.

17. The Wanderer's Chase

Where can I find a place,
With only people—no race?
A world without hatred, without violence to face.
I am a wanderer, searching for peace,
The day I find it, my chase will cease.

18. The Deception Within

I thought the war was over for me,
But it was only a ceasefire.
I thought my heart would speak the truth,
But it turned out to be a liar.

19. Unspoken Truth

Your face tells it all, not your words.
You look thirsty, but I'm not your thirst.
I feel like an option—if not the worst.
And even if you return, it won't be for us.

20. Echoes Of Fear

What should I fear the most?
The voices in my head or whispers from afar?
One tells me to let go, the other pulls me close,
A battle between the past and who we are.
I close my eyes, I cover my ears,
Yet, I tremble—lost in fear.
"It's over," sighed my dream at last,
 And I woke as if I'd seen a ghost from the past.

21. A Question For God

Oh God! Where are you?
If you hear me, then speak.
Not through books, not through signs-
But in words that I can keep.
Oh God! Can't you see?
If you're not blind, then look at me.
Or are you just a ghost-
Roaming minds that are never free?
Oh God! What is your play?
Shrouded in mystery, with countless names.
Are you truth, or just a tale,
Born from minds that blackmail?
Oh God! If this is your game-
Feeding on pain for eternal fame...
Almighty, you may feel.
But you look like a creation of someone insane.

22. I Think

I think my visions are getting blurred,
No matter how I try, it always hurts.
I think I'm losing it—
I hate this feeling, but trust me, I'm not choosing it.
I think they all believe I'm a mess,
Yet when I speak, they say I'm just stressed.
I think they take me for granted,
Though I never asked for the life I never wanted.
I think they don't like the words I say,
Because when I ask them to stay, they just walk away.

23. Caged Dreams

See those birds soaring high,
Masters of their will, proud in the sky.
Watching from my cage, I long to fly.
No wings to lift me — still, I'll try.

See those birds singing with ease,
Not for the chaos but for peace.
Eyes wide open, I drift to sleep,
Healing my soul, piece by piece.

24. Hold On, My Dear

Hold on, my dear!
Just a little longer—I promise, I'll be near.
Can you smile for me? That's all I care,
I know you're waiting—I'm sorry I'm still here.
Hold on, my dear!
The other side is beautiful—just like you,
But you are more than beauty, a truth known by few.
Time isn't on your side, yet you never sought its grace—I always knew.
Hold on, my dear!
It's your magic that makes illusions feel real.
This is your gift so there is nothing to fear.
Your strength speaks loud, all you have to do is hear.
Till then, hold on, my dear.

25. Gone Are the Days

Gone are the days!
When joy was mine in endless ways.
Where is my good ol' smile?
I'll find it again—no matter the trials.
I once chased daylight, now I seek the night,
For when my mind speaks, my heart ignites.
In their endless battle, I lose my sight,
Unsure of what's wrong and what feels right.
So I stand before the mirror and say,
"Hold on—this storm will fade away."
Looking back, I see my past,
Not shrouded in black, but white and vast.
Change is the key, I must survive,
Hold life's hand and take the stride.
Like they say, after darkness shines a ray,
But I won't wait—I'll find my way.
This time, I won't run away.

26. A Dream to Build

The house on that mountain is mine,
I'll take you there for a glass of wine.
I whispered these words in a dream so bright,
Then woke to find only the morning light.
Now I must build what I once only dreamed,
Brick by brick, though distant it seemed.

27. Falling Like the Rain

If I ever fall again, I will fall like the rain,
Drenched in pain, never to be the same.
The thunder will hurl me down to the ground,
You will hear the sound, but I'll never be found.

28. Then What Changed?

Then what changed if you did not?
The time, the date are all moving on.
The night never ends and the sun never dawn,
Restlessness never ceases even if I want.

Then what changed if you did not?
If the fire still burning, why the warmth has gone?
If silence could speak, would it tell me I'm wrong?
Even if it's a lie, I will play along.

Then what changed if you did not?
The words, your voice or the meaning, which I thought.
I am not ready for the truth.
So, tell the *ring* which I bought.

29. Am I Asking Too Much?

Am I asking too much?
Unconditional love, as such.
Holding my soul instead of my hand,
Giving me hope before I rust.

Am I asking too much?
If I want you as my future.
Desperate? Maybe.
But I hate my past, and my present I do not trust.

Am I asking too much?
To be my song.
Walking behind you all the time,
Deaf to others, while listening to you first.

Am I asking too much?
Wanting to be with you.
While I look for you everywhere--
You are the soul, and without you, I am just a husk.

30. Is This What They Call Life?

Is this what they call Life?
Born to love, yet all they do is fight.
Souls trapped in shells.
Smiling faces while they rot inside.

Is this what they call life?
Sharing laughs among all the cries.
Buying happiness and dreams.
Sleeping with nightmares while living with a disguise.

Is this what they call life?
Holding onto faith while God is not nearby.
Building shrines for him.
Amidst bodies falling left and right.

Is this what they call life?
Thinking with their mind while their heart writhe.
Twisting the truth and making it a lie.
Saving the garden by killing butterflies.

Is this what they call life?
Maybe they see and I am blind.
While they seek, I hide.
The show will go on but the death will be on time.